PAINTINGS & DRAWINGS
AT WILTON HOUSE

PHAIDON

Rembrandt: *Portrait of the artist's mother* (Cat. No. 124)

PAINTINGS
AND DRAWINGS
AT WILTON HOUSE

SALISBURY · WILTSHIRE

A SELECTION WITH A FOREWORD BY

SIDNEY, 16TH EARL OF PEMBROKE

WITH 150 ILLUSTRATIONS

PRINTED IN GREAT BRITAIN BY HUNT BARNARD & CO. LTD
AT THE SIGN OF THE DOLPHIN · AYLESBURY · BUCKS

FOREWORD

THE collection at Wilton is one of the oldest in England. No manuscripts have survived to show exactly when it was begun, or what pictures were bought, but it can be dated from the beginning of the reign of James I, when William, 3rd Earl of Pembroke, and his younger brother Philip, 1st Earl of Montgomery (and late 4th Earl of Pembroke as well), were respectively Lord Steward and Lord Chamberlain to the King.

Up to that time, pictures by foreign painters, apart from portraits, were virtually unknown in England. Tudor houses like Wilton, and those built in the reign of James I, contained family portraits, tapestries, hangings and armour. William Herbert, founder of the family and builder of the house on the site of the Abbey given to him by Henry VIII, whose son Edward VI created him Earl of Pembroke, would have had his portrait painted, as well as one of his wife, Ann Parr, sister of Catherine. Their son Henry, 2nd Earl, and his three wives would also have been painted; the famous Mary Sidney, his third wife and mother of the 3rd and 4th Earls, must have sat for the Court painters, though no portraits of her have survived, with the possible exception of a small painting at Penshurst, where she lived as a child. But there are engravings and prints after lost portraits, one by Cornelius Johnson. The Tudor and early Jacobean portraits which surely must have been at Wilton were almost certainly burnt in the fire of 1647, which destroyed so much of the house.

It is supposed, though there are no records of their travels, that William, 3rd Earl, and his brother Philip, on their visits to the Continent, saw paintings by Italian, French, Dutch, Flemish, and German masters, and were duly impressed. It is frustrating not to know whether they bought pictures on their own and had them shipped to England, or whether they employed agents later to buy for them. But there is evidence that by the time James I died in 1625, they already had in their possession some pictures of considerable interest.

The arrival in England of Rubens and Van Dyck added to the growing appreciation of foreign painters, as well as to the desire of the courtiers to be painted by the 'new' artists. The fact that the King, having first claim on their services, commissioned a very large number of Royal portraits, meant that others had to wait their turn. To cope with the commissions, many talented assistants were no doubt taken on in the studios, working under their master's supervision, and to them fell the task of painting much of the backgrounds as well as the dresses.

Van Dyck's large studio was near Blackfriars, and Lord Pembroke and his family, and probably the King as well, must have paid frequent visits to it, though some of the portraits may have been painted inside the Palace of Whitehall, or in Durham House (off the Strand), where Lord Pembroke lived when he did not stay at Wilton with his numerous children.

The great group of the Herbert family, containing ten life-size figures, measures eleven feet in height, and seventeen feet in length; it was begun in 1634–5, and finished in 1636. Perhaps it was painted in Durham House, where it hung for sixteen or seventeen years before being moved to Wilton (which must have presented quite a problem) after Inigo Jones and John Webb had finished building and decorating the 'Double Cube' room, designed to take it and nine other Van Dyck portraits of the family, the King, the Queen, and their three eldest children.

The Civil War undoubtedly reduced the family income considerably, and the cost of rebuilding, decorating and furnishing Wilton must have been enormous, so that Philip was forced to sell much of the collection formed by his father and his uncle. It was perhaps at this time or soon after that the great group of drawings by Holbein, now at Windsor, were sold, only one being retained because the sitter George Nevill, 5th Lord Abergavenny, had been a friend and contemporary Welsh neighbour of the 1st Earl.

Philip, the 5th Earl of Pembroke, did not take a very active part in public life, but he was a member of the Court of Charles II, at whose Coronation in 1661 he bore the Spurs. In 1669 (he died in December of that year) he received an unexpected gift of paintings from Cosimo III, Grand Duke of Tuscany, whom he entertained at Wilton; an account of this visit is given by a Count Magalotti in 'Journal des voyages faits par Come III en 1669' in a manuscript in the Laurentian Library in Florence. The Grand Duke's gift consisted of the following paintings:

The Virgin and Child, St John, and a young woman and child: Andrea del Sarto.
Mary Magdalen: School of Titian.
A Piper: Savoldo.
The Holy Family: Parmegianino.
Offering of the three Kings: School of Paolo Veronese.
A woman with a dog: Correggio.
The Holy Family: Palma Vecchio.
The Ascension: Baldassare Peruzzi.

Gambarini, on page 89 of his catalogue, says that these eight 'were a present to Philip (father of Earl Thomas) from the Duke of Florence, who, when Prince of Tuscany, had been with him at Wilton three or four weeks'.

The first five are still at Wilton; the attributions to Andrea del Sarto and Parmegianino were correct, although the *Piper*, by Savoldo, was given to Giorgione, *Mary Magdalen* to

Sir Anthony van Dyck: *Philip, 4th Earl of Pembroke, and his Family* (Cat. No. 158)

Titian, and the *Offering of the Three Kings* to Veronese. The *Woman with a dog*, if it was by Correggio, was little more than a wreck, and was sold at Christie's on June 22, 1951, lot 16, for £273. The Palma Vecchio and the Peruzzi have disappeared.

Thomas, the brother who succeeded in 1683 as 8th Earl, was a man of very different character; serious-minded, learned, industrious, he was a statesman as well as a patron of the Arts, and he set about the task of restoring the family fortunes, and of adding on a very large scale during the next fifty years to the collection at Wilton. His interests were very wide, a huge library was formed, several hundred pieces of antique sculpture were bought, as well as a famous collection of ancient coins and medals, and the number of paintings by foreign artists was largely increased. At the end of his long life, in 1731, two years before he died, a certain Count Carlo Gambarini of Lucca visited Wilton and compiled the first catalogue under the direction of Lord Pembroke. In his introduction he says that there was an old catalogue (which no longer exists) of the pictures '*collected by the first Earl who lived in four reigns, and by the first two Philips. This Lord [Thomas] has not increased the number, he has only changed many Jerman and Flanders to make a greater variety of Italian Painters. Here are except two or three of above twenty remarkable painters, and of Van Dyke many, because the Great room has only of him, only one of each painter; three quarters of them are by Italian, here being with those that are in London, near three hundred Italian painters ending with the chief disciples of each school, none but such as were alive before the death of Carlo Maratti; of these there were above thirty, they may be easily known by their names to have been the disciples of Carlo Maratti, Carlo Dulci, Giardano of Naples, Albani, and of Cervelli of Venice; these were bespoke when Sir And. Fountaine was in Italy. . . .*'

That is all that is known about the pictures when Earl Thomas was buying, and perhaps exchanging with other collectors in England and on the Continent. He has left no records, so it is not known whether he left the arrangements and the choice to Sir Andrew Fountaine alone, or whether others also acted for him. He may have travelled himself for this purpose; he did go abroad on Government business from time to time, and may have combined business with the pleasure of collecting in foreign studios, galleries and private houses as well as sale rooms, if they existed. The famous Wilton Diptych (now in the National Gallery) '*was given out of the Crown*', so Gambarini records, '*by King James II to the Lord Castlemain when he went Ambassador to Rome, and bought since he dy'd by Thomas, Earl of Pembroke.*'

The 9th Earl, Henry, of whom such an entertaining account is given in Mr James Lees-Milne's books *Earls of Creation*, was chiefly concerned with architecture. But he did not neglect paintings and commissioned Lambert to paint the set of four landscapes of West-comb House, Blackheath, which he had built as a summer retreat from London; views of

Covent Garden and Lincoln's Inn Fields by Scott; and he bought the landscape by Rubens, and the Mieris self-portrait. He also commissioned the busts of himself and his wife, Sir Andrew Fountaine and Martin Folkes by Roubiliac at a cost of ten guineas each.

His son Henry, 10th Earl, patronized Reynolds, by whom there are nine portraits at Wilton; he commissioned from David Morier the series of equestrian portraits, and from Richard Wilson the views of Wilton, as well as buying three small Italian landscapes by him, a Zuccarelli landscape, his own portrait by Batoni, and various portraits of relations and friends.

Three portraits by Beechey were commissioned by him and by his son, George, 11th Earl, to whom General Goldsworthy bequeathed two seascapes by Van der Velde the Younger, a Teniers, a Netscher, a Francken and two Paters (now in the Frick Collection). The additions in the nineteenth century were confined to family portraits by English artists and, with a few exceptions, portraits only have been added in the twentieth century. The most famous painting in the Wilton Collection, the Wilton Diptych, was sold to the National Gallery in 1929 for £90,000; *Judith and Holofernes* by Mantegna was sold in 1917 to the Widener Collection, and is now in Washington. In 1951 and 1960 some ninety very inferior paintings were sold to permit better arrangements in hanging.

There still remains a collection of nearly two hundred and fifty paintings, apart from the ceilings and mural decorations in oil, and the fifty-five gouache paintings of the Spanish *Haute Ecole*, which have survived two world wars and crippling taxation. Like nearly all the houses in the British Isles where there are collections of paintings which can be enjoyed by the public, Wilton can be visited every year from April till October.

January 1, 1968   PEMBROKE

LIST OF PLATES

53. *King Charles I.* Canvas, 50×40 in.

54. *Queen Henrietta Maria.* Canvas, 50×40 in.

55. *Charles, Prince of Wales, James, Duke of York, and Princess Mary, the three eldest children of King Charles I and Queen Henrietta Maria.* Canvas, 48¾×58 in.

56. *Mary Villiers, Duchess of Richmond and Lennox and Mrs Gibson, the Dwarf.* Canvas, 87×51 in.

57. *Elizabeth, Countess of Peterborough.* Canvas, 87×54 in.

58. *The Earl and Countess of Bedford.* Canvas, 51×59 in.

59. *The Countess of Morton and Mrs Killigrew.* Canvas, 51×59 in.

60. *The Duc d'Epernon.* Wood, 12½×9 in.

BARON REIS d'EISENBERG (18th century)

139–140. *Haute Ecole: The Spanish Riding School.* Gouache on paper, backed with wood. Each 10½×15 in.

SCHOOL OF HANS EWORTH (?1520–?1574)

1. *Sir William Herbert, 1st Earl of Pembroke, K.G.* Wood, 79×44 in.

FLEMISH SCHOOL

33. *The Devil tempting Christ.* Wood, 15½×12 in.

FRANS FRANCKEN THE YOUNGER (1581–1642)

49, 52. *Interior of a Picture Gallery.* Wood, 36¾×48½ in.

AFTER GIULIO ROMANO (1492–1546)

90. *Head of Justice.* Red chalk, 14⅜×10⅛ in.

HUGO VAN DER GOES (?1435–1482)

32. *The Adoration of the Shepherds.* Wood, 13×14 in.

JAN GOSSAERT (MABUSE) (?1472–1533)

34. *The Children of Christian II, King of Denmark.* Wood, 12¾×15¾ in.

SIR FRANCIS GRANT, P.R.A. (1810–1873)

30. *Catherine, Countess of Pembroke.* Detail. Canvas, 50×46 in.

31. *Sidney, Lord Herbert of Lea.* Detail. Canvas, 56×43½ in.

SCHOOL OF FRANS HALS (1580–1666)

68. *A Man amusing Children with a Rummel Pot.* Canvas, 43×34 in.

EGBERT VAN HEEMSKERK THE ELDER (1610–1680)

64. *Interior of a Farm House.* Wood, 15¼×19½ in.

JAN VAN DER HEYDEN (1637–1712)

78. *The Church of St Michael, Antwerp.* Wood, 19½×27 in.

PRINCE HOARE (1755–1834)

27. *Lady Charlotte Herbert.* Canvas, 22½×17¾ in.

WILLIAM HOARE (1706–1792)

129. *Henry, 9th Earl of Pembroke.* Red and black chalk, 12¼×10⅞ in.

130. *Mary Fitzwilliam, Countess of Pembroke.* Red and black chalk, 12¼×11⅜ in.

131. *Henry, Lord Herbert.* Black and red chalk, 12×11½ in.

HANS HOLBEIN THE YOUNGER (1497–1543)

41. *Sir George Nevill, 5th Lord Abergavenny.* Black and coloured chalk drawing, 10¾×9¼ in.

SCHOOL OF HOLBEIN THE YOUNGER

40. *King Edward VI.* Wood, 15½×12¼ in.

GERRIT VAN HONTHORST (1590–1656)

65. *Prince Rupert.* Wood, 30×23½ in.

66. *Princess Sophia of Bohemia.* Canvas, 21×18½ in.

FRANK HOWARD (1805–1866)

137. *Prince Michael Woronzow* Canvas, 55×43 in

ITALIAN SCHOOL

103 *Apollo and Marsyas.* Red chalk drawing, 15½×9in.

ALEXANDER KEIRINCX (1600–1652)

61. *Cephalus and Procris.* Wood, 19½×25 in.

GEORGE LAMBERT (1710–1765)

20. *View of Westcombe House, Blackheath.* Canvas, 35×49 in.

21. *View of Westcombe House, Blackheath.* Canvas, 34×48 in.

SIR THOMAS LAWRENCE, P.R.A. (1769–1830)

139. *Count Simon Woronzow.* Canvas, 29×24 in.

SIR PETER LELY (1618–1680)

5. *The Hon. James Herbert and his Wife Jane Spiller.* Canvas, 52×60 in.

8. *Catherine Villiers, Countess of Pembroke, and one of her Daughters.* 52×60 in.

9. *William, 6th Earl of Pembroke.* Canvas, 46×50 in.

10. *Henrietta de Kerouaille, Countess of Pembroke.* Canvas, 50×40 in.

SCHOOL OF SIR PETER LELY

123. *Portrait of a Man.* Canvas, 50 × 40 in.

LUCAS VAN LEYDEN (?1494–1533)

37–38. *The Card Players.* Wood, 14 × 18 in.

CLAUDE LORRAINE (1600–1682)

114. *Landscape with a Tree.* Canvas, 17¼ × 13½ in.

LORENZO LOTTO (?1480–1556)

81. *The Assumption of the Virgin.* Wood, 10 × 21¾ in.

82. *St Anthony the Hermit.* Wood, 13½ × 15¾ in.

BENEDETTO LUTI (1666–1724)

106. *Head of a young Woman.* Black chalk drawing on grey paper, 14½ × 9⅞ in.

MARTIN MAINGAUD (?1660–1725)

119. *Frederick, Prince of Wales, Princess Anne (the Princess Royal), Princess Amelia Sophia Eleanor, and Princess Caroline Elizabeth.* Canvas, 48 × 37½ in.

PHILIPPE MERCIER (1689–1760)

121. *A Musical Family.* Canvas, 25 × 30 in.

PIERO FRANCESCO MOLA (1612–1666)

100. *Bacchus and Ariadne.* Canvas, 19½ × 26 in.

DAVID MORIER (1705–1770)

17. *Henry, 10th Earl of Pembroke.* Canvas, 48 × 60 in.

DANIEL MYTENS (c. 1590–1647)

3. *Philip, 4th Earl of Pembroke and 1st Earl of Montgomery, K.G.* Canvas, 86 × 53 in.

CASPAR NETSCHER (1639–1684)

73. *Portrait of a Man.* Wood, 17¾ × 13½ in.

SCHOOL OF BERNARD VAN ORLEY (c. 1490–1541)

35. *The Virgin and Child, with St Anne and an Angel.* Wood, 35 × 22¼ in.

JACOPO PALMA (IL GIOVANE) (1544–1628)

93. *Soldiers disputing over Christ's Garments.* Canvas, 51 × 60 in.

GIAN PAOLO PANINI (?1691–1764)

111. *Ruins with Figures.* Canvas, 15 × 11 in.

GIANFRANCESCO PENNI (1488–1528)

83. *The Holy Family with the Lamb.* Wood, 11 × 8½ in.

EDWARD PIERCE

142–147. *Hunting Scenes.* Oil on plaster. 30 × 20 ft.

CORNELIS VAN POELENBURGH (?1586–1667)

71. *Landscape with Figures.* Wood, 20½ × 32¼ in.

NICOLAS POUSSIN (?1594–1665)

113. *Two Putti.* Canvas, 14 × 11¾ in.

RAPHAEL (1483–1520)

87. *Head of a Cardinal.* Black chalk drawing, 11⅞ × 9⅜ in.

REMBRANDT VAN RIJN (1606–1669)

Frontispiece. *Portrait of his Mother.* Canvas, 29¾ × 25 in.

SIR JOSHUA REYNOLDS (1723–1792)

18. *Henry, 10th Earl of Pembroke and his son, George, Lord Herbert.* Canvas, 70½ × 94 in.

19. *Elizabeth, Countess of Pembroke.* Canvas, 70½ × 94½ in.

24. *Henry, 10th Earl of Pembroke.* Canvas, 50 × 40 in.

25. *Elizabeth, Countess of Pembroke and her son, George, Lord Herbert.* Canvas, 50 × 40 in.

133. *Augustus Hervey, 3rd Earl of Bristol.* Canvas, 30 × 20 in.

134. *Charles, 3rd Duke of Marlborough.* Canvas, 30 × 26 in.

135. *George, 4th Duke of Marlborough.* Canvas, 50 × 40 in.

136. *Lord Charles Spencer.* Canvas, 50 × 40 in.

JUSEPE RIBERA (1591–1652)

112. *Democritus.* Canvas, 61 × 47 in.

JONATHAN RICHARDSON (1665–1745)

14. *Lady Catherine Herbert and the Hon. Robert Herbert.* Canvas, 50 × 40 in.

15. *Henry, Lord Herbert, afterwards 9th Earl of Pembroke.* Canvas, 50 × 40 in.

AFTER GIULIO ROMANO (1492–1546)

90. *Head of Justice.* Red chalk drawing, 14⅜ × 10⅛ in.

SALVATOR ROSA (1615–1673)

99. *Landscape with Figures.* Canvas, 19 × 25½ in.

SIR PETER PAUL RUBENS (1577–1640)

45. *Landscape with a Shepherd.* Canvas, 27 × 32 in.

46. *Christ, St John and two Angels.* Wood, 37½ × 48 in.

47. *The Martyrdom of S. Vitalis.* Pen and brown ink drawing, 20⅛ × 14⅛ in.

AFTER RUBENS

48. *The Assumption of the Virgin.* Wood, 13½ × 9½ in.

ANDREA SACCHI (1599–1661)

101. *Job with his Wife and Friends.* Canvas, 11 × 14½ in.

G.B. SALVI (SASSOFERRATO), (1609–1685) AND MARIO NUZZI

102. *The Madonna*. Canvas, 29 × 23½ in.

ROELANDT SAVERY (?1576–1639)

62. *St John Preaching*. Copper, 8¼ × 13¼ in.

GIOVANNI GIROLAMO SAVOLDO (?1480–?1548)

88. *A Piper*. Canvas, 20½ × 16 in.

SAMUEL SCOTT (1702–1772)

124. *Lincoln's Inn Fields*. Canvas, 44 × 100 in.
125. *Covent Garden*. Canvas, 44 × 100 in.
126. *Engagement between the Sloop H.M.S.* Blast *and two Spanish Privateers*. Canvas, 32 × 52 in.

LUCA SIGNORELLI (c. 1441–1523)

80. *St John the Divine writing*. Red chalk drawing, 17¼ × 11⅜ in.

GERARD SOEST (?1600–1681)

75. *Portrait of a young Man*. Canvas, 29 × 24½ in.

FRANCESCO SOLIMENA (1657–1747)

108. *The Nativity*. Brown wash drawing over black chalk, 16⅛ × 9¾ in.

SOUTH GERMAN SCHOOL, c. 1500

36. *The Entombment*. Wood, 25½ × 18¼ in.

HENDRICK VAN STEENWIJCK (?1580–1648)

69. *The Liberation of St Peter*. Wood, 11½ × 19½ in.

ATTRIBUTED TO A. TEMPESTA (1555–1630)

95. *A Knight in Armour*. Brown ink drawing with brown wash, 12¼ × 10 in.
96. *Orpheus and a Maiden*. Brown ink drawing over black chalk, 10 × 12¼in.

DAVID TENIERS THE YOUNGER (1610–1690)

63. *The Pipe Smoker*. Wood, 8½ × 11¼ in.

TINTORETTO (1518–1594)

91, 92, 94. *Christ Washing the Disciples' Feet*. Canvas 58 × 99 in.

JAN VAN DER VAART (c. 1647–1727)

12. *Margaret Sawyer, Countess of Pembroke*. Canvas 50 × 40 in.

WILLEM VAN DE VELDE THE YOUNGER (1633–1707)

76. *Shipping in a Calm*. Canvas, 17½ × 25½ in.
77. *Shipping in a Calm*. Canvas, 16 × 20 in.

JAN CORNELISZ VERMEYEN (?1500–1559)

42. *Portrait of a Man*. Wood, 29½ × 24½ in.

CLAUDE-JOSEPH VERNET (1714–1789)

116. *Harbour Scene*. Canvas, 20 × 29 in.

ANTONIO VIVIANI (17th century)

110. *Harbour Scene*. Copper, 11 × 21½ in.

ANTOINE WATTEAU (1684–1721)

120. *A Country Boy*. Black and red chalk drawing, 7⅛ × 3⅞ in.

RICHARD WILSON (1714–1782)

22. *Wilton House from the south-east*. Canvas, 39½ × 57½ in.
23. *Wilton House, south view from the Garden*. Canvas, 39¼ × 49 in.
127. *The Tomb of the Horatii and Curatii*. Canvas, 18¾ × 28¼ in.
128. *Ariccia: a Fallen Tree*. Canvas, 18¾ × 28¾ in.

WILLEM WISSING (1656–1687)

11. *Thomas, 8th Earl of Pembroke*. Canvas, 53 × 40 in.

ARTUS WOLFFORDT (1581–1641)

50. *A Seraglio, or the Bath*. Wood, 22½ × 33¾ in.

JOHANN ZOFFANY (1734–1810)

132. *North Ludlow Bernard*. Canvas, 29½ × 24½ in.

PLATES

The catalogue numbers at the end of the captions refer to the descriptions in *A Catalogue of the Paintings and Drawings in the Collection at Wilton House, Salisbury, Wiltshire, compiled by Sidney, 16th Earl of Pembroke*, published by Phaidon (London and New York), 1968.

1. School of Hans Eworth: *Sir William Herbert, 1st Earl of Pembroke, K.G.* (Cat. No. 146)

2. Sir Anthony van Dyck: *William, 3rd Earl of Pembroke, K.G.* (Cat. No. 159)

3. Daniel Mytens: *Philip, 4th Earl of Pembroke and 1st Earl of Montgomery, K.G.* (Cat. No. 118)

4. Sir Anthony van Dyck: *Philip, 4th Earl of Pembroke, with his second wife, Anne Clifford, his daughter Sophia and her husband Robert, Earl of Carnarvon* (Detail of Cat. No. 158)

5. Sir Peter Lely: *The Hon. James Herbert and his wife Jane Spiller* (Cat. No. 42)

6. Sir Anthony van Dyck: *Charles, Lord Herbert, his wife, Mary Villiers, and his brother Philip, later 5th Earl of Pembroke*
(Detail of Cat. No. 158)

7. Sir Anthony van Dyck: *Philip, 5th Earl of Pembroke*
(Cat. No. 161)

8. Sir Peter Lely: *Catherine Villiers,
Countess of Pembroke* (Cat. No. 44)

9. Sir Peter Lely: *William, 6th Earl of Pembroke*
(Cat. No. 43)

10. Sir Peter Lely: *Henriette de Kerouaille,
Countess of Pembroke* (Cat. No. 41)

11. Willem Wissing:
Thomas, 8th Earl of Pembroke, K.G.
(Cat. No. 134)

12. Jan van der Vaart:
Margaret Sawyer, Countess of Pembroke
(Cat. No. 129)

13. Michael Dahl: *Barbara, Countess of Pembroke*
(Cat. No. 16)

14. Jonathan Richardson: *Lady Catherine Herbert and
the Hon. Robert Herbert* (Cat. No. 74)

15. Jonathan Richardson: *Henry, Lord Herbert, afterwards 9th Earl of Pembroke* (Cat. No. 73)

16. Pompeo Batoni: *Henry, 10th Earl of Pembroke* (Cat. No. 198)

17. David Morier: *Henry, 10th Earl of Pembroke* (Cat. No. 47)

18. Sir Joshua Reynolds: *Henry, 10th Earl of Pembroke, and his son George, Lord Herbert* (Cat. No. 63)

19. Sir Joshua Reynolds: *Elizabeth, Countess of Pembroke* (Cat. No. 64)

20. George Lambert: *View of Westcombe House, Blackheath* (Cat. No. 34)

21. George Lambert: *View of Westcombe House, Blackheath* (Cat. No. 36)

22. Richard Wilson: *Wilton House from the South East* (Cat. No. 83)

23. Richard Wilson: *Wilton House, South View from the Garden* (Cat. No. 85)

24. Sir Joshua Reynolds: *Henry, 10th Earl of Pembroke* (Cat. No. 65)

25. Sir Joshua Reynolds: *Elizabeth, Countess of Pembroke, and her son George, Lord Herbert* (Cat. No. 66)

26. Pompeo Batoni: *George, Lord Herbert* (Cat. No. 199)   27. Prince Hoare: *Lady Charlotte Herbert* (Cat. No. 22)

28. Sir William Beechey: *Lady Herbert* (Cat. No. 7)   29. Sir William Beechey:
Captain Augustus Montgomery (Cat. No. 8)

30. Sir Francis Grant: *Catherine, Countess of Pembroke* (Detail of Cat. No. 20)

31. Sir Francis Grant: *Sidney, Lord Herbert of Lea* (Detail of Cat. No. 19)

32. Hugo van der Goes: *The Adoration of the Shepherds* (Cat. No. 149)

33. Flemish School, XVI or early XVII Century: *The Devil tempting Christ to turn Stone into Bread* (Cat. No. 177)

34. Jan Gossaert: *The Children of Christian II, King of Denmark* (Cat. No. 150)

35. School of Bernard van Orley: *The Virgin and Child with St Anne and an Angel* (Cat. No. 153)

36. South German School: *The Entombment* (Cat. No. 194)

37. Lucas van Leyden: *The Card Players* (Cat. No. 116)

38. Lucas van Leyden: *The Card Players* (Detail of Cat. No. 116)

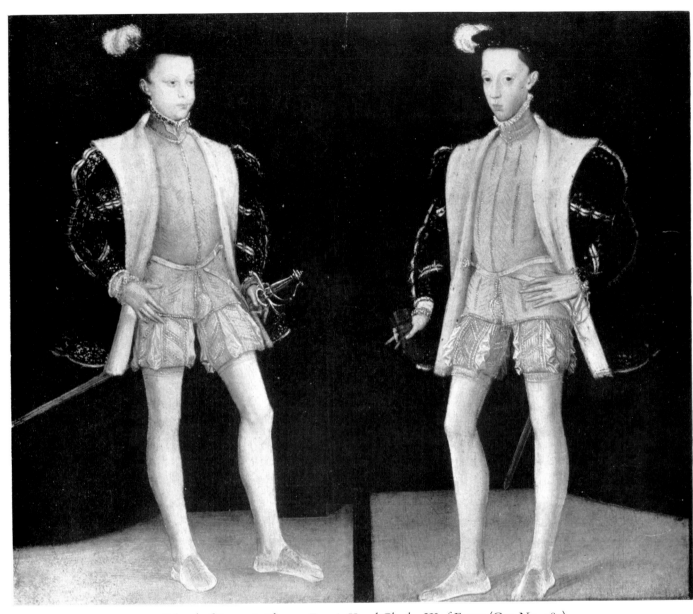

39. School of François Clouet: *Francis II and Charles IX of France* (Cat. No. 180)

40. School of Hans Holbein the Younger: *King Edward VI* (Cat. No. 192)

LORD CROMWELL   HOLBEIN

41. Hans Holbein the Younger: *Sir George Nevill, 5th Lord Abergavenny* (Drawing No. 18)

42. Jan Cornelisz Vermeyen: *Portrait of a Man* (Cat. No. 133)

43. Pieter Brueghel the Younger: 'The Bird Trap' (Cat. No. 143)

44. Jan Brueghel: *Winter Scene in a Village* (Cat. No. 144)

45. Sir Peter Paul Rubens: *Landscape with a Shepherd* (Cat. No. 155)

46. Sir Peter Paul Rubens: *Christ, St John and Two Angels* (Cat. No. 154)

47. Sir Peter Paul Rubens after Federigo Barocci: *The Martyrdom of St Vitalis* (Drawing No. 31)

48. After Sir Peter Paul Rubens: *The Assumption of the Virgin* (Cat. No. 156)

49. Frans Francken the Younger: *Interior of a Picture Gallery* (Cat. No. 148)

50. Artus Wolffordt: *A Seraglio, or the Bath* (Cat. No. 176)

51. Anglo-Dutch School, XVII Century: *King Charles I and Queen Henrietta Maria with William, 3rd Earl of Pembroke, Lord Steward, and his brother Philip, 1st Earl of Montgomery, Lord Chamberlain, inside Whitehall Palace or Durham House* (Cat. No. 141)

52. Frans Francken the Younger: *Interior of a Picture Gallery* (Detail of Cat. No. 148)

54. Sir Anthony van Dyck: *Queen Henrietta Maria* (Cat. No. 165)

53. Sir Anthony van Dyck: *King Charles I* (Cat. No. 164)

55. Sir Anthony van Dyck: *Charles, Prince of Wales, James, Duke of York, and Princess Mary, the three eldest children of King Charles I and Queen Henrietta Maria* (Cat. No. 166)

56. Sir Anthony van Dyck: *Mary Villiers, Duchess of Richmond, and Mrs Gibson, the Dwarf* (Cat. No. 163)

57. Sir Anthony van Dyck: *Elizabeth, Countess of Peterborough* (Cat. No. 170)

58. Sir Anthony van Dyck: *The Earl and Countess of Bedford* (Cat. No. 167)

59. Sir Anthony van Dyck: *The Countess of Morton and Mrs Killigrew* (Cat. No. 168)

60. Sir Anthony van Dyck: *The Duc d'Epernon* (Cat. No. 171)

61. Alexander Keirincx: *Cephalus and Procris* (Cat. No. 151)

62. Roelandt Savery: *St John preaching* (Cat. No. 125)

63. David Teniers the Younger: *The Pipe Smoker* (Cat. No. 174)

64. Egbert van Heemskerk the Elder: *Interior of a Farm House* (Cat. No. 110)

66. Gerrit van Honthorst: *Princess Sophia of Bohemia* (Cat. No. 113)

65. Gerrit van Honthorst: *Prince Rupert* (Cat. No. 112)

67. Abraham Bloemaert: *Shepherd and Shepherdess* (Cat. No. 103)

74. Gerard Ter Borch: *A Young Man seated astride a Rock* (Drawing No. 35)

69. Hendrick van Steenwijck: *The Liberation of St Peter* (Cat. No. 128)

70. Richard Brakenburgh: *Interior of a School* (Cat. No. 105)

71. Cornelis van Poelenburgh: *Landscape with Figures* (Cat. No. 122)

72. Gerard Ter Borch: *Battle Scene* (Cat. No. 104)

73. Caspar Netscher: *Portrait of a Man* (Cat. No. 121)

74. Gerard Ter Borch: *A Young Man seated astride a Rock* (Drawing No. 35)

75. Gerard Soest: *Portrait of a Young Man* (Cat. No. 127)

76. Willem van de Velde the Younger: *Shipping in a Calm* (Cat. No. 130)

77. Willem van de Velde the Younger: *Shipping in a Calm* (Cat. No. 131)

78. Jan van der Heyden: *The Church of St Michael, Antwerp* (Cat. No. 111)

79. Jan Ten Compe: *Almshouses on the River Amstel, Amsterdam* (Cat. No. 106)

80. Luca Signorelli: *St John the Divine writing* (Drawing No. 32)

81. Lorenzo Lotto: *The Assumption of the Virgin* (Cat. No. 209)

82. Lorenzo Lotto: *St Anthony the Hermit* (Cat. No. 208)

83. Gianfrancesco Penni: *The Holy Family with the Lamb* (Cat. No. 215)

84. Cesare da Sesto: *Leda and the Swan* (Cat. No. 224)

85. Andrea del Sarto: *The Virgin and Child, St John, a young Woman and Child* (Cat. No. 221)

86. Andrea del Sarto or Bacchiacca: *Christ bearing the Cross* (Cat. No. 222)

87. Raphael: *Head of a Cardinal* (Drawing No. 26)

88. Giovanni Girolamo Savoldo: *A Piper* (Cat. No. 223)

89. By or after Correggio: *Head of a Putto* (Drawing No. 8)

90. After Giulio Romano: *Head of Justice* (Drawing No. 30)

91. Tintoretto: *Christ washing the Disciples' Feet* (Cat. No. 218)

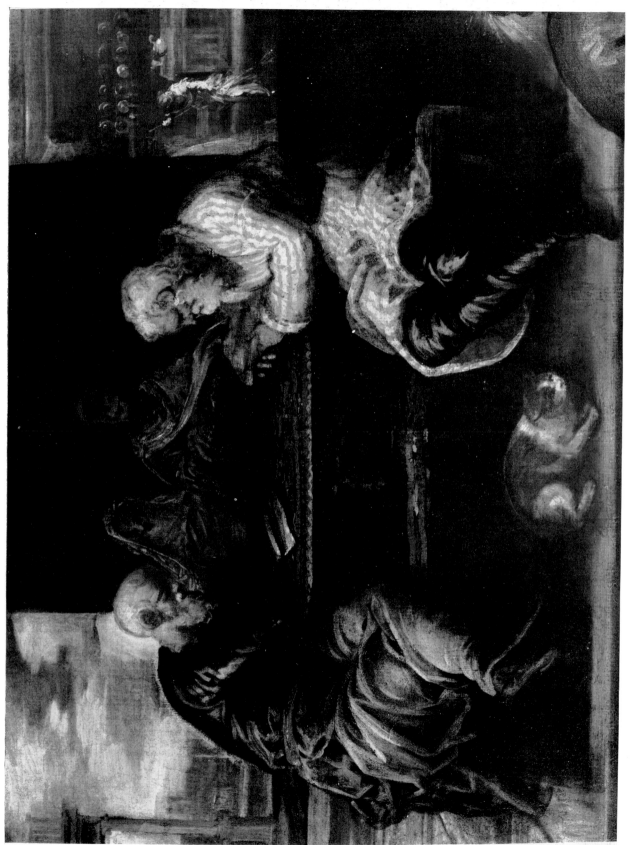

92. Tintoretto: *Christ washing the Disciples' Feet* (Detail of Cat. No. 218)

93. Jacopo Palma: *Soldiers disputing over Christ's Garments* (Cat. No. 213)

94. Tintoretto: *Christ washing the Disciples' Feet* (Detail of Cat. No. 218)

95. Attributed to Antonio Tempesta: *A Knight in Armour on a rearing Horse* (Drawing No. 34A)

96. Attributed to Antonio Tempesta: *Orpheus playing a 'Lira da Braccio', and a Maiden dancing* (Drawing No. 34B)

97. Michelangelo Cerquozzi: *Landscape with Figures* (Cat. No. 203)

98. Pietro Berettini da Cortona: *The Rape of the Sabines* (Cat. No. 204)

99. Salvator Rosa: *Landscape with Figures* (Cat. No. 219)

100. Pier Francesco Mola: *Bacchus and Ariadne* (Cat. No. 212)

101. Andrea Sacchi: *Job with his Wife and Friends* (Cat. No. 220)

102. G. B. Salvi (Sassoferrato) and Mario de' Fiori: *The Madonna* (Cat. No. 220A)

103. Italian (?), XVII Century: *Apollo and Marsyas* (Drawing No. 1)

104. Carlo Dolci: *An Apostle* (Drawing No. 12)

105. Carlo Dolci: *Bust of St John the Divine*
(Drawing No. 13)

106. Benedetto Luti: *Head and shoulders of a young Woman*
(Drawing No. 19)

107. Rosalba Carriera: *A Cupid lying on Clouds* (Drawing No. 6)

108. Francesco Solimena: *The Nativity* (Drawing No. 33)

109. Giuseppe Maria Crespi: *A Group of Market People* (Cat. No. 205)

110. Antonio Viviano: *Harbour Scene* (Cat. No. 227)

III. Gian Paolo Panini: *Ruins with Figures* (Cat. No. 214)

114. Claude Lorraine: *Landscape with a Tree* (Cat. No. 185)

115. Jacques Courtois: *Battle Scene* (Cat. No. 181)

116. Claude-Joseph Vernet: *Harbour Scene* (Cat. No. 189)

117. Antoine Coypel: *A young Zephyr playing a Pipe* (Drawing No 10)

118. Antoine Coypel: *Head of a Woman in a Turban* (Drawing No. 11)

119. Martin Maingaud: *Frederick, Prince of Wales, Princess Anne (the Princess Royal), Princess Amelia Sophia Eleanor, and Princess Caroline Elizabeth* (Cat. No. 193)

120. Antoine Watteau: *A Country Boy, wearing a three-cornered Hat*
(Drawing No. 36)

114. Claude Lorraine: *Landscape with a Tree* (Cat. No. 185)

113. Nicolas Poussin: *Two Putti* (Cat. No. 187)

112. Jusepe Ribera: *Democritus* (Cat. No. 238)

111. Gian Paolo Panini: *Ruins with Figures* (Cat. No. 214)

122. Michael Dahl: *John, 2nd Duke of Montagu,* K.G. (Cat. No. 17)

121. Philippe Mercier: *A Musical Family* (Cat. No. 186)

123. School of Lely: *Portrait of a Man* (Cat. No. 46)

124-125. Samuel Scott: *Lincoln's Inn Fields* (Cat. No. 77) and *Covent Garden* (Cat. No. 78)

126. Samuel Scott: *Engagement between the Sloop H.M.S. 'Blast' and two Spanish Privateers* (Cat. No. 79)

127. Richard Wilson: *The Tomb of the Horatii and Curatii* (Cat. No. 89)

128. Richard Wilson: *Ariccia: A Fallen Tree* (Cat. No. 91)

129. William Hoare: *Henry, 9th Earl of Pembroke*
(Drawing No. 15)

130. William Hoare: *Mary Fitzwilliam, Countess of Pembroke*
(Drawing No. 16)

131. William Hoare: *Henry, Lord Herbert, their son*
(Drawing No. 17)

132. Johann Zoffany: *North Ludlow Bernard* (Cat. No. 93)

133. Sir Joshua Reynolds: *Augustus Hervey, 3rd Earl of Bristol* (Cat. No. 67)

134. Sir Joshua Reynolds: *Charles, 3rd Duke of Marlborough* (Cat. No. 68)

136. Sir Joshua Reynolds: *Lord Charles Spencer* (Cat. No. 70)

135. Sir Joshua Reynolds: *George, 4th Duke of Marlborough* (Cat. No. 69)

138. Sir Thomas Lawrence: *Count Simon Woronzow* (Cat. No. 40)

137. Frank Howard: *Prince Michael Woronzow* (Cat. No. 30)

139–140. Baron Reis d'Eisenberg: *Haute École: The Spanish Riding School* (Cat. No. 2)

141. Baron Reis d'Eisenberg: *Haute École: The Spanish Riding School* (Cat. No. 2)

142. Edward Pierce: *Hunting Scene* (in the Hunting Room)

143. Edward Pierce: *Hunting Scene* (in the Hunting Room)

144. Edward Pierce: *Hunting Scene* (in the Hunting Room)

145. Edward Pierce: *Hunting Scene* (in the Hunting Room)

146. Edward Pierce: *Hunting Scene* (in the Hunting Room)

147. Edward Pierce: *Hunting Scene* (in the Hunting Room)

148. Andien de Clermont: '*Singerie*' (Ceiling in the Colonnade Room)